D0493215

FOR THE BEST MUM EVER

Isobel Carlson

summersdale

FOR THE BEST MUM EVER

Copyright © Summersdale Publishers Ltd, 2017

With research by Rebecca Collins

Images © Shutterstock

All rights reserved.

No part of this book may be reproduced by any means, nor transmitted, nor translated into a machine language, without the written permission of the publishers.

Condition of Sale
This book is sold subject to the condition that it shall not, by way of trade or otherwise, be lent, resold, hired out or otherwise circulated in any form of binding or cover other than that in which it is published and without a similar condition including this condition being imposed on the subsequent purchaser.

Summersdale Publishers Ltd
46 West Street
Chichester
West Sussex
PO19 1RP
UK

www.summersdale.com

Printed and bound in China

ISBN: 978-1-84953-980-7

Substantial discounts on bulk quantities of Summersdale books are available to corporations, professional associations and other organisations. For details contact Nicky Douglas by telephone: +44 (0) 1243 756902, fax: +44 (0) 1243 786300 or email: nicky@summersdale.com.

To..

From..

CONTENTS

BEING
A MUM

Being a mum means more than simply creating
a new life; it means being bestowed with the gift
of an incredible love for another human being, a
love different from any other. That love blossoms
in the first few days of your child's life and it
feels as if it cannot possibly get any stronger.
Yet it is a love that never stops growing.

The moment a child is born, the mother is also born.

BHAGWAN SHREE RAJNEESH

BABY

Where did you come from, baby dear?
Out of the everywhere into the here.

Where did you get your eyes so blue?
Out of the sky as I came through.

What makes the light in them sparkle and spin?
Some of the starry spikes left in.

Where did you get that little tear?
I found it waiting when I got here.

What makes your forehead so smooth and high?
A soft hand stroked it as I went by.

What makes your cheek like a warm white rose?
Something better than any one knows.

Whence that three-cornered smile of bliss?
Three angels gave me at once a kiss.

Where did you get that pearly ear?
God spoke, and it came out to hear.

Where did you get those arms and hands?
Love made itself into hooks and bands.

Feet, whence did you come, you darling things?
From the same box as the cherub's wings.

How did they all just come to be you?
God thought about me, and so I grew.

But how did you come to us, you dear?
God thought of you, and so I am here.

GEORGE MacDONALD

You gave me the
greatest gift a person
can give: life.

Hack

SMALL ITEM RETRIEVAL SYSTEM

Keeping tiny objects and small children apart from each other is one of the main preoccupations of motherhood in the early years. But even if you don't have small children and the spectre of A&E doesn't loom large anymore, you will find this hack a life saver for finding minute treasured things.

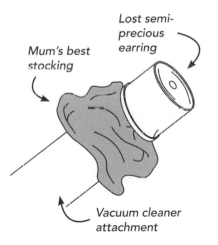

Mum's best stocking

Lost semi-precious earring

Vacuum cleaner attachment

When you drop something small and cannot find it, grab your vacuum cleaner and a pair of tights. Slip the tights over the vacuum nozzle and fix in place with an elastic band. Run the vacuum over the area where you think you dropped your item and, with a bit of luck, the item will be sucked onto the tights where you can pick it off with ease.

CHOCOLATE BANANA BREAD

Bananas are one of the first foods a child gets to eat as they are easy to prepare, easily digested and naturally sweet and filling. Bananas remain a comfort food for many throughout childhood and into adulthood. They are combined here with chocolate to make a sweet and delicious loaf, which is guaranteed to be a big hit with the whole family, at any age and for any occasion.

INGREDIENTS:

110 g softened butter

225 g golden caster sugar

2 eggs

4 small ripe bananas

90 ml milk

1 tsp vanilla extract

275 g plain flour

1 tsp bicarbonate of soda

150 g milk chocolate

PREPARATION METHOD:

Preheat the oven to 180°C/
350°F/gas mark 4. Grease a
20 cm x 12.5 cm loaf tin.

In a large mixing bowl, beat
together the butter and sugar
until light and fluffy. Add
the eggs, bananas, milk and
vanilla extract, and stir well.

Sift in the flour and bicarbonate
of soda and stir.

Cut each square of chocolate
into approx. four pieces and add
to the mixture. Fold the mixture
until it is well combined.

Transfer the mixture into the
loaf tin and bake for 50–55
minutes until golden brown,
checking after 45 minutes.

A Nursery Darling

A Mother's breast:
Safe refuge from her childish fears,
From childish troubles, childish tears,
Mists that enshroud her dawning years!
See how in sleep she seems to sing
A voiceless psalm – an offering
Raised, to the glory of her King
In Love: for Love is Rest.

A Darling's kiss:
Dearest of all the signs that fleet
From lips that lovingly repeat
Again, again, the message sweet!
Full to the brim with girlish glee,
A child, a very child is she,
Whose dream of heaven is still to be
At Home: for Home is Bliss.

LEWIS CARROLL

IT MAKES
ME HAPPY
THAT YOU ARE
WITH ME FOR
EVERY STEP
THAT I TAKE.

Biology is the least of
what makes someone
a mother.

OPRAH WINFREY

'MOTHERING' SUDOKU

Every row, column and mini-grid must contain
all the letters to the word mothering.

N				E			R	
	O		T		H			G
	E	I			R	T	H	O
O		G	I		N	E		
			T					
		E	H		M	G		N
I	G	T	R			M	N	
M			E		I		O	
	H			M				I

TO A LITTLE CHILD

Clear eyes of heaven's chosen hue
When not a cloud is seen above
To fleck the warm untroubled blue,
A little laughing face of love;

A boundless energy of life
In dimpled arms and rosy feet;
No breath of care, no touch of strife,
Has dulled thy glad heart's rhythmic beat.

So girt about with golden light,
By shadows still so little vexed,
That many a weary anxious wight
Grows in thy presence less perplexed.

Our smiles come at thy fairy beck,
Frowns pass away at thy caress;
When thy soft arms are round my neck
I feel God's wondrous tenderness.

ANNIE MATHESON

NO MATTER WHAT
LIFE THROWS AT ME,
I KNOW YOU WILL
ALWAYS BE THERE.

CELEBRATIONS

There are many milestones to celebrate in family
life: birthdays, anniversaries and new adventures
such as starting nursery, school or a new job.
Motherhood is about change and growth. One of
the most joyous aspects of being a mum is seeing
your child develop, overcome and achieve, and being
able to celebrate those precious moments together.

The art of mothering
is to teach the art of
living to children.

ELAINE HEFFNER

A Seed

See how a Seed, which Autumn flung down,
And through the Winter neglected lay,
Uncoils two little green leaves and two brown,
With tiny root taking hold on the clay
As, lifting and strengthening day by day,
It pushes red branchless, sprouts new leaves,
And cell after cell the Power in it weaves
Out of the storehouse of soil and clime,
To fashion a Tree in due course of time;
Tree with rough bark and boughs' expansion,
Where the Crow can build his mansion,
Or a Man, in some new May,
Lie under whispering leaves and say,
'Are the ills of one's life so very bad
When a Green Tree makes me deliciously glad?'
As I do now. But where shall I be
When this little Seed is a tall green Tree?

WILLIAM ALLINGHAM

You make
every day
special.

Hack

WRAP IT UP FOR LESS

Christmas and birthdays can be expensive times but if you want to save some money they also offer an opportunity to let your creative juices flow. Comics and newspaper pages make for colourful and unusual present wrapping. This works best with old fashioned children's comics or broadsheets, but magazines, old book pages or comic book pages work too. The wrapped gifts can be tied together with brightly contrasting string or ribbon, or to save more money and continue the theme, the ribbon could also be made out of strips of colourful magazine paper. A great idea for the bookworm in your family and it'll save you a bomb!

Inexpensive yet quirky wrapping

Lovely present underneath

CHOCOLATE CELEBRATION CAKE

Birthdays mark the passage of time and celebrate life.
They offer a chance for the family to get together to
celebrate another year since the birth of a child. This
sumptuous chocolate cake is suitable for young and
old alike and very easy to make, which makes it a
perfect highlight to any family birthday tea party.

INGREDIENTS:

For the cake:

150 g butter

275 g dark brown sugar

2 eggs, beaten

225 g plain flour

50 g cocoa powder

2 tsp baking powder

½ tsp bicarbonate of soda

225 ml milk

2 tsp vanilla extract

For the chocolate icing:

200 g plain chocolate

200 ml double cream

PREPARATION METHOD:

Preheat the oven to 180°C/350°F/
gas mark 4.

Grease two 20 cm round sandwich
tins and line with baking paper.

In a large bowl, beat together the butter
and sugar, then gradually add the eggs.
Sift in the flour, cocoa powder, baking
powder and bicarbonate of soda and fold
to combine. Slowly add the milk and
vanilla extract, stirring continuously.

Pour half of the mixture into each tin,
and bake for 30 minutes. Remove from
the oven and allow to cool completely.

Meanwhile, heat the chocolate and cream
in a small pan over a low heat until the
chocolate is melted, then remove from the
heat. Whisk together until smooth and thick.
Leave to cool and thicken for 1 hour.

Remove the cakes from their tins.
Spread chocolate icing over one cake,
then place the other cake on top.
Spread the remaining icing over the
whole cake with a palette knife.

MY DELIGHT AND THY DELIGHT

My delight and thy delight
Walking, like two angels white,
In the gardens of the night:

My desire and thy desire
Twining to a tongue of fire,
Leaping live, and laughing higher:

Thro' the everlasting strife
In the mystery of life.

Love, from whom the world begun
Hath the secret of the sun.

Love can tell, and love alone,
Whence the million stars were strewn,
Why each atom knows its own,
How, in spite of woe and death,
Gay is life, and sweet is breath:

This he taught us, this we knew,
Happy in his science true,
Hand in hand as we stood
'Neath the shadows of the wood,
Heart to heart as we lay
In the dawning of the day.

ROBERT BRIDGES

NO ONE EVER OUTGROWS THE NEED FOR A MOTHER'S LOVE.

JANETTE OKE

BIRTHDAY PUZZLE

Can you guess my birthday?

The day before yesterday I was 20 years old. Next year I will be 23. This fact is true for only one day in the year. What is the date of my birthday?

A PRAYER FOR A MOTHER'S BIRTHDAY

Lord Jesus, Thou hast known
A mother's love and tender care:
And Thou wilt hear, while for my own
Mother most dear I make this birthday prayer.

Protect her life, I pray,
Who gave the gift of life to me;
And may she know, from day to day,
The deepening glow of Life that comes from Thee.

As once upon her breast
Fearless and well content I lay,
So let her heart, on Thee at rest,
Feel fears depart and troubles fade away.

Her every wish fulfill;
And even if Thou must refuse
In anything, let Thy wise will
A comfort bring such as kind mothers use.

Ah, hold her by the hand,
As once her hand held mine;
And though she may not understand
Life's winding way, lead her in peace divine.

I cannot pay my debt
For all the love that she has given;
But Thou, love's Lord, wilt not forget
Her due reward, – bless her in earth and heaven.

HENRY van DYKE

You are in
all my best
memories.

ON THE ROAD

Children of all ages are interested in the world around them and love the fun of the journey just as much as the final destination. Travelling in daily life, whether to school, to visit family or to the shops, is not just a means of getting somewhere; together you can make it an adventure.

TO TRAVEL IS TO LIVE.

HANS CHRISTIAN ANDERSEN

The Child's Quest

My mother twines me roses wet with dew;
Oft have I sought the garden through and through;
I cannot find the tree whereon
My mother's roses grew.
Seek not, O child, the tree whereon
Thy mother's roses grew.

My mother tells me tales of noble deeds;
Oft have I sought her book when no one heeds;
I cannot find the page, alas,
From which my mother reads.
Seek not, O child, to find the page
From which thy mother reads.

My mother croons me songs all soft and low,
Through the white night where little breezes blow;
Yet never when the morning dawns,
My mother's songs I know.
Seek not, O child, at dawn of day
Thy mother's songs to know.

FRANCES SHAW

YOU MAKE
THE ORDINARY
MAGICAL.

ICE LOLLY DRIP-CATCHER

It might seem a strange thing to have in your day-trip travel bag but after reading this hack you will not want to travel without cake cases, especially on hot days when your family is likely to want a cool, refreshing treat.

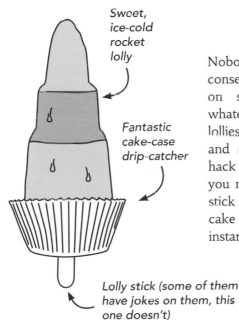

Sweet,
ice-cold
rocket
lolly

Fantastic
cake-case
drip-catcher

Lolly stick (some of them
have jokes on them, this
one doesn't)

Nobody is immune to the messy consequences of melting ice lollies on sweltering summer days, whatever their age. Dripping ice lollies can mean sticky fingers and sticky clothes. This clever hack will put an end to that. All you need to do is poke the lolly stick through the middle of the cake case and this will create an instant drip-catcher.

EDAMAME HUMMUS

Nobody likes hungry travelling with no food stops in sight. Sometimes it is hard to predict how long a journey is going to take and on those occasions it is good to have an easy-to-prepare snack with you for keeping your family's hunger at bay. A pot of edamame is the perfect solution for traffic jams or long journeys, and even older family members will enjoy popping the beans from their shells.

For longer journeys or as part of a lunch stop, edamame hummus is easy to prepare in advance and delicious with vegetable sticks or pitta bread.

INGREDIENTS:

225 g shelled edamame

60 g tahini paste

60 ml water

½ tsp lemon zest

juice of 1 lemon

1 clove of garlic (crushed)

¾ tsp salt

½ tsp ground cumin

¼ tsp ground coriander seeds

2 tbsp extra-virgin olive oil

1 tbsp chopped parsley

PREPARATION METHOD:

Boil the beans in water for 4–5 minutes. Or, alternatively, heat the beans in a covered microwave-proof dish in 2 cm of water for 2–3 minutes.

Place the edamame, tahini, water, lemon zest, lemon juice, garlic, salt, cumin and coriander in a food processor and blend until smooth. Slowly drizzle in the olive oil and continue to blend until all the ingredients have been absorbed.

Transfer into a bowl and stir in the parsley. For travelling, use a plastic pot with lid.

Serve with carrot sticks, cucumber, breadsticks or pitta.

From a Railway Carriage

Faster than fairies, faster than witches,
Bridges and houses, hedges and ditches;
And charging along like troops in a battle,
All through the meadows the horses and cattle:
All of the sights of the hill and the plain
Fly as thick as driving rain;
And ever again, in the wink of an eye,
Painted stations whistle by.

Here is a child who clambers and scrambles,
All by himself and gathering brambles;
Here is a tramp who stands and gazes;
And there is the green for stringing the daisies!
Here is a cart run away in the road
Lumping along with man and load;
And here is a mill and there is a river:
Each a glimpse and gone for ever!

ROBERT LOUIS STEVENSON

I HAVEN'T BEEN EVERYWHERE, BUT IT'S ON MY LIST.

SUSAN SONTAG

LE DÉJEUNER SUR L'HERBE

Solve the clues correctly and the letters in the shaded
squares will spell the name of an essential component
of summertime lunch stops on long journeys.

1. Traditional snippet of advice
2. Resistance to movement
3. Vegetables left for Rudolf at Christmas
4. Andy Murray's job?
5. Copy, mimic
6. Mimicking moggy

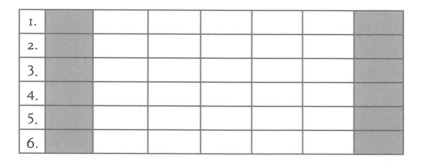

1.						
2.						
3.						
4.						
5.						
6.						

FROM

A Boy's Song

Where the mowers mow the cleanest,
Where the hay lies thick and greenest,
There to track the homeward bee,
That's the way for Billy and me.

Where the hazel bank is steepest,
Where the shadow falls the deepest,
Where the clustering nuts fall free,
That's the way for Billy and me.

Why the boys should drive away
Little sweet maidens from the play,
Or love to banter and fight so well,
That's the thing I never could tell.

But this I know, I love to play
Through the meadow, among the hay;
Up the water and over the lea,
That's the way for Billy and me.

JAMES HOGG

You make the getting there just as much fun as the destination.

HOLIDAYS

Sand, sunshine, lazy days, games with brothers and sisters, visits to museums, games at the park: these are the building blocks of family holiday memories. Family vacations are a time for experiencing new places together, or for just relaxing and being away from the hubbub of everyday life.

A MOTHER'S HAPPINESS IS LIKE A BEACON, LIGHTING UP THE FUTURE BUT REFLECTED ALSO ON THE PAST IN THE GUISE OF FOND MEMORIES.

HONORÉ DE BALZAC

My Magic Shell

Pink shells, white shells, and
shells coloured blue;
Smooth shells, crinkled shells,
old shells and new;
Striped shells, and plain
shells lift by the tide;
My shell is magic – the sea
sings inside.

ANONYMOUS

You make holidays
such fun!

Hack

TOILET TUBE SPEAKER

Of course, holidays aren't all about sunshine. Imagine waking up to pelting rain and howling winds... a day indoors looms and you need some lively music to cheer everyone up. However, there's a snag to your plan: there isn't a CD player or radio, and you didn't pack any speakers. With this clever hack, a lack of speakers won't stop you from being able to brighten up the day with some happy tunes for your family.

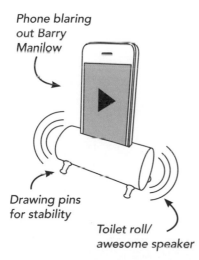

Phone blaring
out Barry
Manilow

Drawing pins
for stability

Toilet roll/
awesome speaker

All you need is a smartphone and a toilet roll. Cut a slot in the toilet roll big enough to fit the phone, and stop the tube from rolling away by sticking some drawing pins into it to act as feet (if no drawing pins are available, an alternative could be two clothes pegs attached either end of the toilet roll). Not only have you amplified the sound but you've also made a cheap docking station.

CHINESE BARBECUE CHICKEN

The word 'barbecue' is synonymous with summer. It conjures up the smells, sounds and tastes associated with outdoor eating on balmy evenings: charcoal smoke, spitting meat, chargrilled vegetables, fresh salad and fruit.

This dish mixes the taste of summer with that of the Orient and is great for al fresco dining. It is best started a couple of hours ahead of serving as the meat benefits from being marinated. For optimum taste, leave overnight.

INGREDIENTS:

3 cm piece of fresh ginger

1 clove of garlic

2 tbsp clear honey

2 tsp Chinese five spice

2 tsp soy sauce

1 tbsp sesame oil

4 chicken drumsticks

4 chicken wings

PREPARATION METHOD:

Peel and grate the ginger, peel and
crush the garlic, then mix with
the honey, spices, soy and oil.

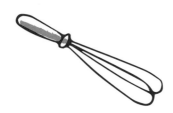

Place the chicken in an ovenproof
dish, coat with the honey mixture and
leave to marinate for at least half an
hour in the fridge (leave overnight
in the fridge for best results).

Place the chicken on the barbecue
over medium-hot coals and cook
for about 20 minutes, making
sure you cook the chicken all the
way through. To check, pierce a
drumstick with a skewer: if the
juices are still pink, carry on cooking.
This dish can be cooked in an oven
(180°C/350°F/gas mark 4 for 30
minutes in an ovenproof dish).

Alternatively, if you want to be
sure that the chicken is cooked
thoroughly but still has the authentic
barbecue taste, part cook the
chicken for 20 minutes in the
oven and finish for a further 10
minutes on the barbecue coals.

CHILD AND MOTHER

O Mother-my-Love, if you'll give me your hand,
And go where I ask you to wander,
I will lead you away to a beautiful land, –
The Dreamland that's waiting out yonder.
We'll walk in a sweet posie-garden out there,
Where moonlight and starlight are streaming,
And the flowers and the birds are filling the air
With the fragrance and music of dreaming.

There'll be no little tired-out boy to undress,
No questions or cares to perplex you,
There'll be no little bruises or bumps to caress,
Nor patching of stockings to vex you;
For I'll rock you away on a silver-dew stream
And sing you asleep when you're weary,
And no one shall know of our beautiful dream
But you and your own little dearie.

And when I am tired I'll nestle my head
In the bosom that's soothed me so often,
And the wide-awake stars shall sing, in my stead,
A song which our dreaming shall soften.
So, Mother-my-Love, let me take your dear hand,
And away through the starlight we'll wander, –
Away through the mist to the beautiful land, –
The Dreamland that's waiting out yonder.

EUGENE FIELD

WE TRAVEL NOT TO ESCAPE LIFE, BUT FOR LIFE NOT TO ESCAPE US.

ANONYMOUS

MUSICAL
CRYPTOGRAM

Solve the cryptogram and hear this
catchy summertime song.

Z	H	'	U	H		D	O	O		J	R	L	Q	J		R	Q	
		'									O							

D		V	X	P	P	H	U		K	R	O	L	G	D	B
		U													

Beside the Idle Summer Sea

Beside the idle summer sea,
And in the vacant summer days,
Light Love came fluting down the ways,
Where you were loitering with me.

Who have not welcomed even as we,
That jocund minstrel and his lays
Beside the idle summer sea
And in the vacant summer days?

We listened, we were fancy-free;
And lo! in terror and amaze
We stood alone – alone and gaze
With an implacable memory
Beside the idle summer sea.

WILLIAM ERNEST HENLEY

LET YOUR
MEMORY BE YOUR
TRAVEL BAG.

ALEKSANDR SOLZHENITSYN

Holidays with
you end where good
memories start.

NATURE

Children are natural explorers and have a
fearless interest in the great outdoors, and our
inner explorer stays with us well into adulthood.
The natural world can be a vast playground of
discovery for you and your family, whether in the
countryside, on the beach or in woodland. It is a
place of adventure, imagination and exploration.

The sun does not shine for a few trees and flowers, but for the wide world's joy.

HENRY WARD BEECHER

A Child in the Garden

When to the garden of untroubled thought
I came of late, and saw the open door,
And wished again to enter, and explore
The sweet, wild ways with stainless bloom inwrought,
And bowers of innocence with beauty fraught,
It seemed some purer voice must speak before
I dared to tread that garden loved of yore,
That Eden lost unknown and found unsought.

Then just within the gate I saw a child, –
A stranger-child, yet to my heart most dear;
He held his hands to me, and softly smiled
With eyes that knew no shade of sin or fear:
'Come in,' he said, 'and play awhile with me;'
'I am the little child you used to be.'

HENRY van DYKE

KEEP THE BUGS AT BAY

Being out and about and enjoying the great outdoors can be a pleasure shared by all the family but that doesn't mean that we want to share our food and drink with nature's creatures, particularly the flying and stinging ones.

Cupcake case (unused)

Bug-free beverage

This hack provides some protection against the constant wafting of flies and wasps from the sweet drinks that accompany outdoor eating. All you need are some cupcake cases packed in with your picnic. Take one cupcake case per drink, and cut a small X into the centre (do this before you leave home). Before dishing out the drinks, poke a straw through the hole and place the upside-down cupcake case and straw into the cup of drink. Then you and your children will be free to enjoy your drink without bugs.

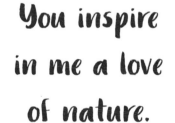

You inspire
in me a love
of nature.

TUNA, POTATO AND EGG SALAD

This salad is perfect for outdoor eating, whether just in the garden on warm sunny days or out and about as part of a picnic. It is packed with protein, it is delicious and also easy to prepare.

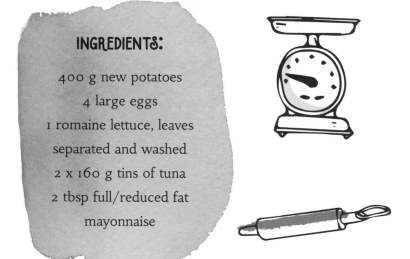

INGREDIENTS:

400 g new potatoes

4 large eggs

1 romaine lettuce, leaves separated and washed

2 x 160 g tins of tuna

2 tbsp full/reduced fat mayonnaise

OPTIONAL: To make an authentic tuna Niçoise, add some or all of the following ingredients to your salad: cooked green beans, cherry tomatoes cut in half, a handful of black olives and drained and rinsed anchovy fillets.

PREPARATION METHOD:

Bring a pan of water to the boil. Add
the potatoes and the eggs, and cook
the eggs for 7–10 minutes (depending
on how hard boiled you like your eggs)
and the potatoes for 10–15 minutes.

When cooked for your desired
amount of time, scoop the eggs
out of the pan and run under
cold water until cool. Drain the
potatoes and also leave to cool.

Cut the potatoes in half, and peel
the eggs and cut into quarters.

Arrange the lettuce leaves in
shallow bowls (or in plastic tubs
for a picnic). Scatter over the
potatoes and egg quarters.

Flake the tuna into chunks and scatter
over the salad. Mix the mayonnaise
and 1 tbsp cold water in a bowl until
smooth. Drizzle over the salad.

A Baby Running Barefoot

When the bare feet of the baby beat across the grass
The little white feet nod like white flowers in the wind,
They poise and run like ripples lapping across the water;
And the sight of their white play among the grass
Is like a little robin's song, winsome,
Or as two white butterflies settle in the cup of one flower
For a moment, then away with a flutter of wings.

I long for the baby to wander hither to me
Like a wind-shadow wandering over the water,
So that she can stand on my knee
With her little bare feet in my hands,
Cool like syringa buds,
Firm and silken like pink young peony flowers.

D. H. LAWRENCE

IF LOVE IS SWEET
AS A FLOWER
THEN MY MOTHER
IS THAT SWEET
FLOWER OF LOVE.

STEVIE WONDER

THE WEIRD
AND WONDERFUL
WORDS OF NATURE

Our language contains many weird and wonderful
words and the language of nature is no exception.
What is the correct definition of the following?

Frondescence
a. The smell of nature
b. Green foliage
c. Mildew

Hyemation
a. The passing of winter
b. An allergic reaction
    to wasp stings
c. The coming of spring

Aestivation
a. The passing of summer
b. To slow down
    during hot months
c. Winter flowering

Moonglade
a. The path the moon
    follows in the sky
b. The track of
    moonlight on water
c. A flower that blooms
    only at night

Ombrophobous
a. Non-flowering plants
b. Meat-eating plants
c. Rain-hating plants

A MOTHER HOLDS
HER CHILDREN'S HANDS
FOR A WHILE AND THEIR
HEARTS FOREVER.

ANONYMOUS

NATURE, THE GENTLEST MOTHER

Nature, the gentlest mother
Impatient of no child,
The feeblest or the waywardest –
Her admonition mild

In forest and the hill
By traveller is heard,
Restraining rampant squirrel
Or too impetuous bird.

How fair her conversation
A summer afternoon –
Her household, her assembly;
And when the sun goes down

Her voice among the aisles
Incite the timid prayer
Of the minutest cricket,
The most unworthy flower.

When all the children sleep
She turns as long away
As will suffice to light her lamps;
Then, bending from the sky,

With infinite affection
And infiniter care,
Her golden finger on her lip,
Wills silence everywhere.

EMILY DICKINSON

YOU SHOW
ME HOW TO
LISTEN TO THE
MUSIC OF
THE EARTH.

FUN AND GAMES

Enjoying sports and games with your family has many benefits, even when they have grown up. Not only does sport bring a smile to your face – it's true, the feel-good hormone serotonin is released with exercise – but it's a great way of communing with children of all ages, be it a game of rounders, or a jog or cycle ride with your grown-up children.

A mother's heart is the child's classroom.

HENRY WARD BEECHER

YOU MAKE ME
REALISE THAT
I CAN ACHIEVE
ANYTHING.

THE SONG OF THE UNGIRT RUNNERS

We swing ungirded hips,
And lightened are our eyes,
The rain is on our lips,
We do not run for prize.
We know not whom we trust
Nor whitherward we fare,
But we run because we must
Through the great wide air.

The waters of the seas
Are troubled as by storm.
The tempest strips the trees
And does not leave them warm.
Does the tearing tempest pause?
Do the tree-tops ask it why?
So we run without a cause
'Neath the big bare sky.

The rain is on our lips,
We do not run for prize.
But the storm the water whips
And the wave howls to the skies.
The winds arise and strike it
And scatter it like sand,
And we run because we like it
Through the broad bright land.

CHARLES HAMILTON SORLEY

SCRUMPTIOUS SMOOTHIES

Smoothies are a good source of energy. As well as being tasty for adults and children alike, they provide essential vitamins and minerals necessary for a healthy body and mind. They are so easy to make and can be pre-prepared for taking outdoors. All that you need is a blender, fruit, ice and milk or yoghurt and the possible combinations of flavours are endless. Here are just a few.

KIWI AND MELON SMOOTHIE

Kiwis are packed full of Vitamin C and here the acid bite of the kiwi blends perfectly with the smoothness of the melon.

INGREDIENTS:

½ honeydew melon

1 kiwi fruit

1 apple

2 tsp honey

4 ice cubes

PREPARATION METHOD:

Peel and slice the melon and kiwi fruit. Peel the apple and core it, then cut into small chunks. Place all of the ingredients into the blender and blend until smooth.

BANANA AND RASPBERRY SMOOTHIE

The sometimes sharp flavour of raspberries is
offset by the sweetness of the pineapple juice
in this wonderfully refreshing smoothie.

INGREDIENTS:

2 bananas

240 ml pineapple juice

120 ml natural yoghurt

175 g raspberries

4 ice cubes

PREPARATION METHOD:

Place all of the ingredients
into the blender and
blend until smooth.

TROPICAL SMOOTHIE

If you're out and about and being active, this mild,
sweet smoothie is the perfect energy boost.

INGREDIENTS:

5 strawberries

100 g mango flesh

1 small banana

200 ml apple juice

PREPARATION METHOD:

Wash the strawberries carefully
and cut off the green leafy tops.
Peel and chop the mango. Place
all of the ingredients into the
blender and blend until smooth.

The Swing

How do you like to go up in a swing,
Up in the air so blue?
Oh, I do think it the pleasantest thing
Ever a child can do!

Up in the air and over the wall,
Till I can see so wide,
Rivers and trees and cattle and all
Over the countryside –

Till I look down on the garden green,
Down on the roof so brown –
Up in the air I go flying again,
Up in the air and down!

ROBERT LOUIS STEVENSON

I love that you don't always let me win. But I love it more when you do!

GLOW-IN-THE-DARK BOWLING

During the cold winter months it can be hard to be motivated to get out and about for outdoor family games, especially in the dark early evenings. This hack will tempt you out for a novel version of tenpin bowling which is that bit more exciting – and cheaper – than going to your local bowling alley.

You need: six glowsticks, six plastic water bottles full of water (with their labels removed), a ball heavy enough to knock down the bottles (for example, a basketball or football) and a pen and paper to keep score.

Pour a little water out of each bottle and pop a glowstick into each one. Set up your 'bowling pins' in a triangle formation and take it in turns to knock them down with your ball. This activity is not only a lot of fun; it will get you all moving and having family time together.

Water-filled
bottles

Glowsticks

A mother's love
perceives no
impossibilities.

CORNELIA PADDOCK

CARD GAME WORD QUEST

Make as many words of four or more letters as possible from the nine letters below. In making each word, each letter may be used only once and each word must contain the central letter A. The name of a popular family card game can be found using all nine letters.

Proper names do not count.

Scoring: 30 words very good; 40 words excellent; over 60 words genius.

K	E	W
E	A	M
N	T	R

The Baby's Dance

Dance little baby, dance up high,
Never mind baby, mother is by;
Crow and caper, caper and crow,
There little baby, there you go;
Up to the ceiling, down to the ground,
Backwards and forwards, round and round;
Dance little baby, and mother shall sing,
With the merry coral, ding, ding, ding.

ANN TAYLOR

We don't stop playing
because we grow old,
we grow old because
we stop playing.

GEORGE BERNARD SHAW

I CAN DO
ANYTHING WITH
YOU BY MY SIDE.

RELAXING

Motherhood is extremely rewarding but it can
also be a busy time. It is important to find space
in the daily schedule to recharge and enjoy
precious me-time, whether that be in the form
of a warm bath, a good book in a cosy corner
or coffee and cake in a favourite coffee shop.

A MOTHER'S
HEART IS A
PATCHWORK
OF LOVE.

ANONYMOUS

I LOVE TO
SEE YOU SMILE.

From Perfect Woman

She was a phantom of delight
When first she gleam'd upon my sight;
A lovely apparition, sent
To be a moment's ornament;
Her eyes as stars of twilight fair;
Like twilight's, too, her dusky hair;
But all things else about her drawn
From May-time and the cheerful dawn;
A dancing shape, an image gay,
To haunt, to startle, and waylay.

I saw her upon nearer view,
A Spirit, yet a Woman too!
Her household motions light and free,
And steps of virgin liberty;
A countenance in which did meet
Sweet records, promises as sweet;
A creature not too bright or good
For human nature's daily food;
For transient sorrows, simple wiles,
Praise, blame, love, kisses, tears, and smiles.

WILLIAM WORDSWORTH

To a Lady, Who Said It Was Sinful to Read Novels

To love these Books, and harmless Tea,
Has always been my foible,
Yet will I ne'er forgetful be
To read my Psalms and Bible.

Travels I like, and Hist'ry too,
Or entertaining Fiction;
Novels and Plays I'd have a few,
If sense and proper diction.

I love a natural harmless Song,
But I cannot sing like Handel;
Depriv'd of such resource, the tongue
Is sure employ'd – in scandal.

CHRISTIAN MILNE

I LOVE THE
TIME WE SPEND
TOGETHER.

TAKE IT EASY TRANQUIL TEA

Little beats the pleasure of half an hour or so with a
good book and a soothing drink in a favourite cosy
chair, away from the chaos of life. This tea is ideal
for unwinding and de-stressing after a busy day.

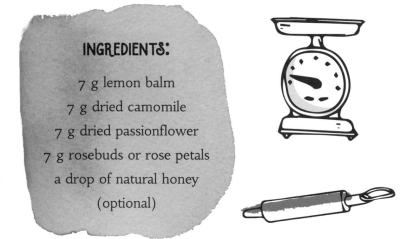

INGREDIENTS:

7 g lemon balm

7 g dried camomile

7 g dried passionflower

7 g rosebuds or rose petals

a drop of natural honey

(optional)

PREPARATION METHOD:

In a bowl, combine the dried herbs and mix well.
Add a spoon of the mixture into the tea strainer or
a spoon per person into a teapot. Cover with boiling
water and allow to infuse for 5 minutes.

Add a drop of natural honey for sweetness if desired.

YOU'RE MY BEST FRIEND AS WELL AS MY MUM.

Leisure

What is this life if, full of care,
We have no time to stand and stare.

No time to stand beneath the boughs
And stare as long as sheep or cows.

No time to see, when woods we pass,
Where squirrels hide their nuts in grass.

No time to see, in broad daylight,
Streams full of stars, like skies at night.

No time to turn at Beauty's glance,
And watch her feet, how they can dance.

No time to wait till her mouth can
Enrich that smile her eyes began.

A poor life this is if, full of care,
We have no time to stand and stare.

WILLIAM HENRY DAVIES

All you need
is love. But a
little chocolate now
and then doesn't hurt.

CHARLES M. SCHULZ

PUBLICATION DATE PUZZLE

Put the following ten much-loved novels in the order of publication, from earliest to most recent.

1. *Little Women*

2. *The Girl on the Train*

3. *Gone with the Wind*

4. *The Great Gatsby*

5. *Madame Bovary*

6. *The Time Traveler's Wife*

7. *Tess of the D'Urbervilles*

8. *Rebecca*

9. *Jane Eyre*

10. *Lady Chatterley's Lover*

TWENTY-FIRST-CENTURY BATHTIME READING

Before power showers were standard in every home, the bath was purely functional. It was simply the means to clean and it was used by everyone. The bath has now evolved to become a sanctuary for relaxation. Many a busy mum loves to take a warm bath for relaxation and solitude and the time as an opportunity to read without disruption.

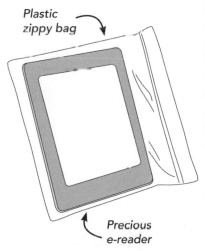

Plastic zippy bag

Precious e-reader

However, since the invention of e-readers, this simple pleasure may be more difficult to indulge in if your latest page-turner is not in paper form. This hack will allow you to read in the bath once again, with no risk of destroying your entire library with one slip of the hand.

Simply place your e-book reader into a plastic zip-lock food bag and you can read on without worry.

Time you enjoy
wasting is not
wasted time.

MARTHE TROLY-CURTIN

Mother's Evening Prayer

O gentle presence, peace and joy and power;
O Life divine, that owns each waiting hour,
Thou Love that guards the nestling's faltering flight!
Keep Thou my child on upward wing tonight.
Love is our refuge; only with mine eye
Can I behold the snare, the pit, the fall:
His habitation high is here, and nigh,
His arm encircles me, and mine, and all.
O make me glad for every scalding tear,
For hope deferred, ingratitude, disdain!
Wait, and love more for every hate, and fear
No ill, – since God is good, and loss is gain.
Beneath the shadow of His mighty wing;
In that sweet secret of the narrow way,
Seeking and finding, with the angels sing:
'Lo, I am with you alway,' – watch and pray.
No snare, no fowler, pestilence or pain;
No night drops down upon the troubled breast,
When heaven's aftersmile earth's tear-drops gain,
And mother finds her home and heav'nly rest.

MARY BAKER EDDY

FOOD

From that moment of birth, children will look to their mum as the main provider of food. As your children grow up, they will associate your cooking with home and comfort. Meal times feature largely in both day-to-day family life and on special occasions: they are a time for closeness, sharing news and just being together.

LIFE EXPECTANCY WOULD GROW BY LEAPS AND BOUNDS IF GREEN VEGETABLES SMELLED AS GOOD AS BACON.

DOUG LARSON

A Few Rules for Beginners

Babies must not eat the coal
And they must not make grimaces,
Nor in party dresses roll
And must never black their faces.

They must learn that pointing's rude,
They must sit quite still at table,
And must always eat the food
Put before them – if they're able.

If they fall, they must not cry,
Though it's known how painful this is;
No – there's always Mother by
Who will comfort them with kisses.

KATHERINE MANSFIELD

YOUR
CAKES
ARE THE
BEST,
EVEN THE
DISASTER
ONES!

HAPPY PIE

Who can resist a smile when taking a bite of happy pie?
This classic dish, packed with apples and spices, won't fail to
spread cheer and could even grow to be a family favourite.

INGREDIENTS:

For the pastry:
340 g plain flour
pinch of salt
150 g butter
1 tbsp caster sugar
1 egg, beaten
1 tsp water

For the filling:
700 g cooking apples,
peeled, cored and sliced
juice of ½ lemon

100g sultanas
(optional)
75 g brown sugar
grated zest of 1 orange
pinch of ground cinnamon
pinch of freshly grated
nutmeg
1 tbsp milk

To serve:
1 tbsp caster sugar

PREPARATION METHOD:

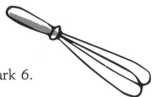

Preheat oven to 200°C/400°F/gas mark 6.

In a large bowl, combine the flour, salt and butter, and rub together until the mixture resembles breadcrumbs. Add the sugar, egg and a splash of water to form dough.

Knead dough on a lightly floured work surface and roll out gently.

Use two thirds of the pastry to line a 1 litre pie dish.

In a bowl, sprinkle the apples with the lemon juice, and layer the apples, sultanas (if desired), sugar, orange zest, cinnamon and nutmeg in the pie dish.

Use the remaining pastry to form the pie lid, brushing the edges with milk and pressing together. Brush the top with milk. Before baking make a slit in the centre of the pie lid to let steam escape.

Bake for 30 minutes, or until golden brown. Once the pie is out of the oven, sprinkle caster sugar on top and serve.

From A Recipe for Salad

To make this condiment, your poet begs
The pounded yellow of two hard-boiled eggs;
Two boiled potatoes, passed through kitchen sieve,
Smoothness and softness to the salad give.
Let onion atoms lurk within the bowl,
And, half suspected, animate the whole.
Of mordant mustard add a single spoon,
Distrust the condiment that bites so soon;
But deem it not, thou man of herbs, a fault,
To add a double quantity of salt;
Four times the spoon with oil from Lucca crown,
And twice with vinegar, procured from town;
And, lastly, o'er the flavoured compound toss
A magic soupçon of anchovy sauce.
O green and glorious! O herbaceous treat!
'T would tempt the dying anchorite to eat.

SYDNEY SMITH

KETCHUP POLISH

Polishing pans with ketchup may sound crazy but it really does work. Amazingly, this staple sauce has the power to buff up your pots and pans.

Spread a thin layer of ketchup onto the offending piece of cookware and rub it in. Leave it to work for 30 minutes (keeping the pan away from anybody who might want to taste some delicious red sauce). A substance found in ketchup called acetic acid will react with the oxides that have caused your pans to discolour. When you come to wipe it off you will reveal the sparkling surface of the pan as if it were new!

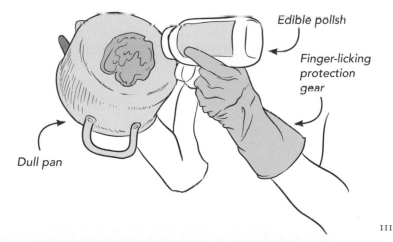

Edible polish

Finger-licking protection gear

Dull pan

WORRIES GO DOWN
BETTER WITH SOUP.

JEWISH PROVERB

FEED
BETWEEN
THE LINES

A word that describes once-a-year, aerodynamic sweet treats can be inserted in the blank line so that, reading downwards, eight three-letter words are formed. What is that sweet treat?

A	J	A	I	H	S	P	A
E	M	D	E	M	Y	A	H

A Home Song

I read within a poet's book
A word that starred the page:
'Stone walls do not a prison make,
Nor iron bars a cage!'

Yes, that is true; and something more
You'll find, where'er you roam,
That marble floors and gilded walls
Can never make a home.

But every house where Love abides,
And Friendship is a guest,
Is surely home, and home-sweet-home:
For there the heart can rest.

HENRY van DYKE

WITHOUT ICE CREAM, THERE WOULD BE DARKNESS AND CHAOS.

DON KARDONG

When I'm sad,
you always cook
my favourite dish.

BATHTIME AND BEDTIME

The rituals of bathtime and bedtime are so important to children, and continue to be so throughout life. This precious time in the evening provides an opportunity for you and your child to wind down after a hectic day and enjoy some quiet time: perhaps talking through the day, reading together or enjoying a bedtime snack and drink.

A mother's arms
are made of tenderness
and children sleep
soundly in them.

VICTOR HUGO

BATHTIME IS
ALWAYS FUN
WITH YOU.

THE WASHING
AND DRESSING

Ah! why will my dear little girl be so cross,
  And cry, and look sulky, and pout?
To lose her sweet smile is a terrible loss,
  I can't even kiss her without.

You say you don't like to be wash'd and be dress'd,
  But would you not wish to be clean?
Come, drive that long sob from your dear little breast,
  This face is not fit to be seen.

If the water is cold, and the brush hurts your head,
  And the soap has got into your eye,
Will the water grow warmer for all that you've said?
  And what good will it do you to cry?

It is not to tease you and hurt you, my sweet,
But only for kindness and care,
That I wash you, and dress you, and make you look neat,
And comb out your tanglesome hair.

I don't mind the trouble, if you would not cry,
But pay me for all with a kiss;
That's right – take the towel and wipe your wet eye,
I thought you'd be good after this.

ANN TAYLOR

SLEEPY HOT CHOCOLATE

This sweet, soothing hot chocolate is great for a pre-bedtime wind-down drink for anyone of any age (remembering to brush teeth after drinking).

INGREDIENTS:

1 tbsp cocoa powder
1 tsp golden syrup
¼ tsp ground cinnamon
½ tsp vanilla extract
180 ml milk
(dairy or non-dairy)

To serve (optional):
cream
marshmallows
extra cinnamon

PREPARATION METHOD:

Mix together the cocoa powder, golden syrup, cinnamon, vanilla and 2 tbsp of milk in a mug. Use a fork or a mini whisk until the mixture resembles a thick syrup.

Over a medium heat, warm the rest of the milk until it begins to bubble, then pour it into the mug with the chocolate syrup and stir thoroughly.

For an extra indulgence, add whipped cream, an extra sprinkle of cinnamon and/or marshmallows to the drink.

For orange chocolate lovers, substitute ground cinnamon for grated orange zest.

Nurse's Song

When the voices of children are heard on the green,
And laughing is heard on the hill,
My heart is at rest within my breast,
And everything else is still.

'Then come home, my children, the sun is gone down,
And the dews of night arise;
Come, come leave off play, and let us away
Till the morning appears in the skies.'

'No, no, let us play, for it is yet day,
And we cannot go to sleep;
Besides, in the sky the little birds fly,
And the hills are all cover'd with sheep.'

'Well, well, go and play till the light fades away,
And then go home to bed.'
The little ones leapèd, and shoutèd, and laugh'd
And all the hills echoèd.

WILLIAM BLAKE

You make me feel
safe at night.

AROUND THE WORLD
IN A BATHTUB

Children are busy taking in new information all the time and often don't even realise they are doing so. So why not combine learning with cleaning? All you need is a shower curtain with the map of the world on it so that the members of your family can absorb geography as they sit in the bath or dream of world travel as they scrub in the shower.

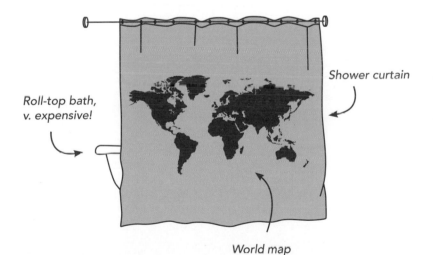

Shower curtain

Roll-top bath, v. expensive!

World map

Always kiss your children goodnight, even if they are already asleep.

H. JACKSON BROWN Jr

Bedtime

'Come, children, put away your toys;
　　Roll up the kite's long line;
The day is done for girls and boys –
　　Look, it is almost nine!
Come, weary foot, and sleepy head,
　Get up, and come along to bed.'

The children, loath, must yet obey;
　　Up the long stair they creep;
Lie down, and something sing or say
　　Until they fall asleep,
To steal through caverns of the night
Into the morning's golden light.

We, elder ones, sit up more late,
　　And tasks unfinished ply,
But, gently busy, watch and wait –
　　Dear sister, you and I,
To hear the Father, with soft tread,
　Coming to carry us to bed.

GEORGE MacDONALD

FLOATING WORDBUILDER

The letters of two words containing ten letters
have been numbered one to ten. Solve the clues
to discover a traditional bathtime friend.

Letters 3, 5 and 7 give us a place to sleep.
Letters 1, 5 and 7 is the colour of anger.
Letters 7, 8, 10 and 5 is a member of the nobility.
Letters 9, 8, 1 and 5 together spells the remedy for ill health.
Letters 6, 2 and 4 will bring forth a genie from a bottle.

| 1 | 2 | 3 | 4 | 5 | 6 | | 7 | 8 | 9 | 10 |

THERE NEVER
WAS A CHILD SO
LOVELY, BUT HIS
MOTHER WAS GLAD TO
GET HIM ASLEEP.

RALPH WALDO EMERSON

I LOVE IT
WHEN YOU TUCK
ME IN AT NIGHT.

STRIDING OUT

A lot of pleasure comes from walking together as a family, whether it be a wander around town on a Saturday afternoon, a walk in the country, or a stroll along a blustery beach or coastal path. There's a lot to see and share together and perhaps the promise of a hot chocolate and a slice of cake in a café too.

I still find each day too short for all the thoughts I want to think, all the walks I want to take.

JOHN BURROUGHS

I Love the South-west Wind

I love the south-west wind, or low and loud,
And not the less when sudden drops of rain
Moisten my pallid cheek from ebon cloud,
Threatening soft showers again,
That over lands new ploughed and meadow grounds
Summer's sweet breath unchain,
And wake harmonious sounds.

Rich music breathes in summer's every sound;
And in her harmony of vivid greens,
Woods, meadows, hedge-rows, corn fields, all around
Much beauty intervenes
Filling with harmony the ear and eye;
While o'er the mingling scenes
Far spreads the laughing sky.

JOHN CLARE

CHOCOLATE ORANGE FLAPJACK

Flapjacks are a great sweet snack for on-the-go days and family walks. The oats release their energy slowly, and the sugar from the golden syrup provides a rapid energy boost to keep you going for longer. This recipe also has an added tang of citrus and a dark chocolate decadence.

INGREDIENTS:

250 g margarine or
unsalted butter

150 g soft brown sugar

110 g golden syrup

500 g porridge oats

juice of ½ orange

zest of 1–2 oranges

150 g dark chocolate

PREPARATION METHOD:

Preheat the oven to
180°C/350°F/gas mark 4.

Melt the butter in a microwave-
proof bowl in the microwave or
over a warm pan of water and add
it to the sugar and golden syrup
in a separate bowl. Mix well. Add
the oats and mix thoroughly.

Add the orange juice and zest to the
mixture and fold together. Break
the chocolate into pieces and stir in.
Allow the mixture to cool to room
temperature. Meanwhile, grease
a 30 cm x 20 cm baking tray.

Once the mixture is cooled,
smooth it over the greased baking
tray and press down firmly
with the back of a spoon.

Cook for 30 minutes, or until the
top has turned golden brown in
colour. Remove from the oven and
allow to cool. Once cooled, cut the
mixture into chunks ready for eating.

FROM WALKING

To walk is by a thought to go;
To move in spirit to and fro;
To mind the good we see;
To taste the sweet;
Observing all the things we meet
How choice and rich they be.

To note the beauty of the day,
And golden fields of corn survey;
Admire each pretty flow'r
With its sweet smell;
To praise their Maker, and to tell
The marks of his great pow'r.

To fly abroad like active bees,
Among the hedges and the trees,
To cull the dew that lies
On ev'ry blade,
From ev'ry blossom; till we lade
Our minds, as they their thighs.

Observe those rich and glorious things,
The rivers, meadows, woods, and springs,
The fructifying sun;
To note from far
The rising of each twinkling star
For us his race to run.

A little child these well perceives,
Who, tumbling in green grass and leaves,
May rich as kings be thought,
But there's a sight
Which perfect manhood may delight,
To which we shall be brought.

While in those pleasant paths we talk,
'Tis that tow'rds which at last we walk;
For we may by degrees
Wisely proceed
Pleasures of love and praise to heed,
From viewing herbs and trees.

THOMAS TRAHERNE

DAYLIGHT MEASURE

Here's a hack for when you fear that you and your family have wandered a little too far away from civilisation and the sun is not far off disappearing over the horizon. You can put your mind at ease once you have learnt the skill of estimating the amount of daylight left using nothing other than your bare hand.

Hold your arm parallel to the horizon with your fingers straight and your thumb tucked in. Line your index finger with the bottom of the sun and count how many finger-widths there are between the sun and the horizon. Each finger equals roughly 15 minutes of daylight. If there are only five minutes of daylight left then it is time to shout: 'last one back is a rotten egg!'

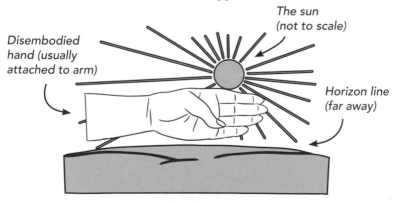

*The sun
(not to scale)*

*Disembodied
hand (usually
attached to arm)*

*Horizon line
(far away)*

GOOD THINGS ARE COMING DOWN THE ROAD. JUST DON'T STOP WALKING.

ROBERT WARREN PAINTER Jr

MISSING WORDS

A four-letter word completes the first word or phrase and
starts the second. So in 'baby _ _ _ _ cloth' the missing
word would be 'face', making 'baby face' and 'facecloth'.

1. Back _ _ _ _ watch

2. Foot _ _ _ _ room

3. Cottage _ _ _ _ _ cake

4. Home _ _ _ _ flow

5. Hand _ _ _ _ body

Answer to a Child's Question

Do you ask what the birds say? The Sparrow, the Dove,
The Linnet and Thrush say, 'I love and I love!'
In the winter they're silent – the wind is so strong;
What it says, I don't know, but it sings a loud song.
But green leaves, and blossoms, and sunny warm weather,
And singing, and loving – all come back together.
But the Lark is so brimful of gladness and love,
The green fields below him, the blue sky above,
That he sings, and he sings; and for ever sings he –
'I love my Love, and my Love loves me!'

SAMUEL TAYLOR COLERIDGE

A JOURNEY OF A THOUSAND MILES BEGINS WITH A SINGLE STEP.

LAO TZU

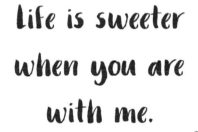

Life is sweeter
when you are
with me.

FUN
TOGETHER

One of the highlights of living with children is
the laughter and the fun that they bring into the
household. Family life is never dull with the jokes,
the tea-time conversations, the games and the
silliness. Even when your children have grown up and
return to the family home for visits, within moments
of their return the fun and laughter resumes.

Sing out loud in the car even, or especially, if it embarrasses your children.

MARILYN PENLAND

To My Mother

Gentlest of critics, does your memory hold
(I know it does) a record of the days
When I, a schoolboy, earned your generous praise
For halting verse and stories crudely told?
Over these childish scrawls the years have rolled,
They might not know the world's unfriendly gaze;
But still your smile shines down familiar ways,
Touches my words and turns their dross to gold.

More dear to-day than in that vanished time
Comes your nigh praise to make me proud and strong.
In my poor notes you hear Love's splendid chime,
So unto you does this, my work belong.
Take, then, a little gift of fragile rhyme:
Your heart will change it to authentic song.

JOYCE KILMER

You know
how to brighten
up even the
dullest days.

HERBY BREAD

There's nothing like the hands-on process of making bread and the feeling of satisfaction in creating something that is usually bought in a shop (but tastes far nicer when made at home). This bread is great for making, and eating, with your family. It could even form part of a rainy day, indoor picnic.

INGREDIENTS:

30 g fresh yeast

225 ml warm water

450 g strong plain flour

2 tsp salt

2 tbsp olive oil

*Also needed for
the herby version:*

1 tbsp basil

1 tsp onion powder

1 tsp garlic powder

1 tsp oregano

PREPARATION METHOD:

Stir the yeast into the warm
water until it dissolves.

Sift the flour and salt onto a work
surface, and make a well in the centre.
Pour in the dissolved yeast and olive
oil. Gradually mix in the flour and, if
baking the herby version, add in the
remaining ingredients, and when well
mixed, knead the dough for 8 minutes.

Put the dough in a lightly floured
bowl. Cover with a damp tea towel
and leave to rise in a warm place.
This will take about 1 hour.

Preheat the oven to
230°C/450°F/gas mark 8.

Mould the dough into a loaf shape and set
aside in a warm place until it's 1½ times
its original size. Bake for 10 minutes.

Reduce the heat to 190°C/375°F/
gas mark 5 and bake for a further
45 minutes. Remove to a cooling
rack and let cool before eating.

MR NOBODY

I know a funny little man,
As quiet as a mouse,
Who does the mischief that is done
In everybody's house!
There's no one ever sees his face,
And yet we all agree
That every plate we break was cracked
By Mr Nobody.

'Tis he who always tears out books,
Who leaves the door ajar,
He pulls the buttons from our shirts,
And scatters pins afar;
That squeaking door will always squeak,
For prithee, don't you see,
We leave the oiling to be done
By Mr Nobody.

He puts damp wood upon the fire,
That kettles cannot boil;
His are the feet that bring in mud,
And all the carpets soil.
The papers always are mislaid,
Who had them last but he?
There's not one tosses them about
But Mr Nobody.

The finger marks upon the door
By none of us are made;
We never leave the blinds unclosed,
To let the curtains fade.
The ink we never spill; the boots
That lying round you see
Are not our boots, – they all belong
To Mr Nobody.

ANONYMOUS

BEANBAG CAMERA TRIPOD

The family day out or get-together would not be complete without the group photo to capture the moment for the mantelpiece. If you're a fan of photography on a budget, you'll appreciate this beanbag tripod, or unipod to be more precise. It's sturdy, simple to use and will cost you next to nothing to make.

Simply fill a cloth sack or bag with dried lentils or beans, and sew the ends together or tie them shut. Place it on the ground, or nestle it on a fence or rock, set the timer, run into shot and say a collective 'cheese' and farewell to wonky and blurry photos.

Fancy SLR (aren't you Mrs Moneybags?!)

Mini beanbag

MOTHERHOOD: ALL LOVE BEGINS AND ENDS THERE.

ROBERT BROWNING

INDOOR
GAMES
ANAGRAMS

The following anagrams conceal a number
of fun family indoor games which are perfect
for rainy days or Sunday afternoons.

1. Dad is keen, eh?

2. Thus, rear tune

3. Aged Rambo

4. Car shade

5. Gus cooked duck

FROM
Little Things

Little drops of water,
Little grains of sand,
Make the mighty ocean
And the pleasant land.
Little deeds of kindness,
Little words of love,
Make our world an Eden
Like the Heaven above.

JULIA CARNEY

YOUR LOVE
KNOWS NO
BOUNDS.

SOLUTIONS

'Mothering' Sudoku, p.17:

N	T	H	O	E	G	I	R	M
R	O	M	T	I	H	N	E	G
G	E	I	M	N	R	T	H	O
O	M	G	I	R	N	E	T	H
H	I	N	G	T	E	O	M	R
T	R	E	H	O	M	G	I	N
I	G	I	R	H	O	M	N	E
M	N	R	E	G	I	H	O	T
E	H	O	N	M	T	R	G	I

Birthday Puzzle, p.31: 31st December

Le Déjeuner sur l'herbe, p.44:

P	R	O	V	E	R	B
I	N	E	R	T	I	A
C	A	R	R	O	T	S
N	E	T	W	O	R	K
I	M	I	T	A	T	E
C	O	P	Y	C	A	T

Musical Cryptogram, p.57:

'We're All Going on a Summer Holiday'

The Weird and Wonderful Words of Nature, p.70:

1. B   2. A   3. B   4.B   5. C

Card Game Word Quest, p.86:

Main word is 'Newmarket'

Publication Date Puzzle, p.100:

Jane Eyre, 1847
Madame Bovary, 1857
Little Women, 1868
Tess of the D'Urbervilles, 1891
The Great Gatsby, 1925
Lady Chatterley's Lover, 1928
Gone with the Wind, 1936

Rebecca, 1938
The Time Traveler's Wife, 2003
The Girl on the Train, 2015

Feed Between the Lines, p.113: Pancake

Floating Wordbuilder, p.128: Rubber duck

Missing Words, p.140:

1. Back stop / stop watch

2. Football / ballroom

3. Blue cheese / cheesecake

4. Homework / workflow

5. Handsome / somebody

Indoor Games Anagrams, p.154:

1. Hide and Seek

2. Treasure Hunt

3. Board Game

4. Charades

5. Duck, Duck, Goose

If you're interested in finding out more about our books, find us on Facebook at Summersdale Publishers and follow us on Twitter at @Summersdale.

www.summersdale.com

Image credits © Freepik; © Shutterstock: Natali Zakharova / NottomanVi / abracada / Le Panda / Inna Ogando / Olga Olmix /Anastasiya Samolovova / nednapa / Color Brush / Katja Gerasimova / Mur / Artnis / Yulia Sribna / silm / Angie Makes / Ozerina Anna / Bukhavets Mikhail